1 Red
2 Green
3 Blue
4 Orange
5 Yellow
6 Pink
7 Brown
8 Cream

1 Cream
2 Green
3 Blue
4 Orange
5 Yellow
6 Pink
7 Black

1 Red
2 Green
3 Light Blue
4 Orange
5 Yellow
6 Pink
7 Brown

Printed in the USA
CPSIA information can be obtained
at www.ICGtesting.com
LVHW070957141223
766499LV00025B/258